S0-BJO-561

The Snail and the Cherry Tree

To Laurel Amber

Published by the Press Syndicate of the University of Cambridge
The Pitt Building, Trumpington Street, Cambridge CB2 2RU, UK
© text, Joan Dalgleish 1990   © illustrations, Gillian Campbell 1990
Typeset in 16/18pt Century Old Style   Printed in Hong Kong by Colorcraft
First published 1990
Originated, developed and produced by
Margaret Hamilton Books Pty Ltd P.O. Box 28, Hunters Hill NSW 2110, Australia
National Library of Australia cataloguing-in-publication data:
Dalgleish, Joan.
The snail and the cherry tree.
ISBN 0 521 40003 1.
I. Campbell, Gillian. II. Title.
A823.3
British Library cataloguing-in-publication data applied for

The Snail
and the
Cherry Tree

Joan Dalgleish
illustrated by Gillian Campbell

CAMBRIDGE UNIVERSITY PRESS
Cambridge
New York Port Chester Melbourne Sydney
in association with
MARGARET HAMILTON BOOKS

Valley Farm lay silent under the night frost, and a cold wind moaned in the branches of the giant pine trees. Drifts of smoke rose from the fuel-stove chimney in the old wooden farmhouse.

The house dog and cat lay sleeping on their sheepskin. The farmer and his wife made a large mound under the feather quilt on the big bed. Beside them, their two children made a smaller mound under the quilt on the small bed.

A faint sound from the grain shed reached the dog's ear. He growled softly. The cat stretched.

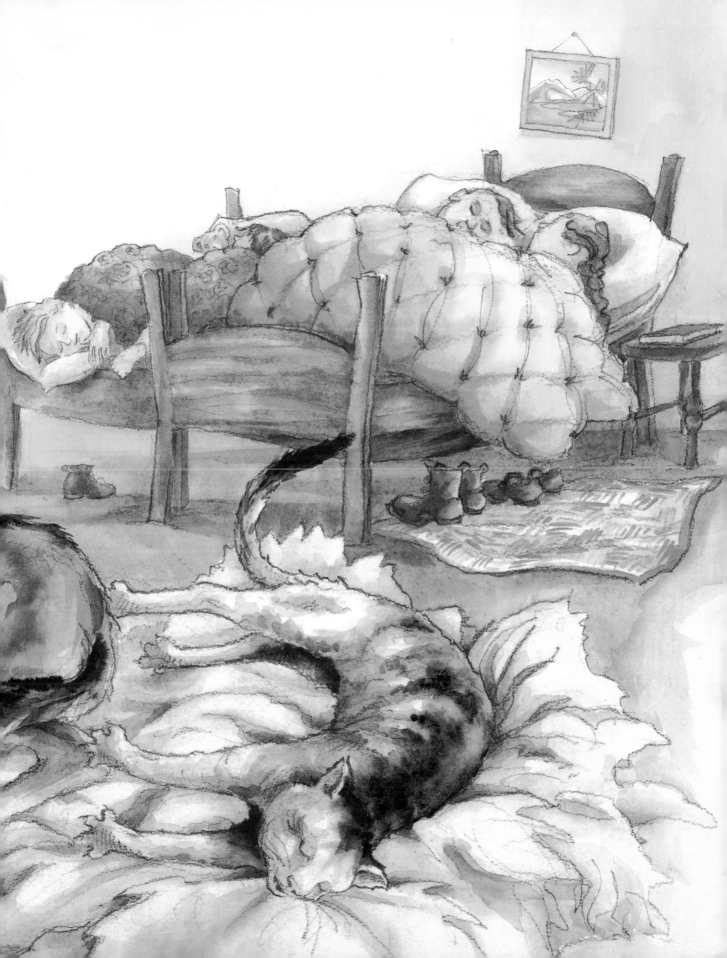

Inside the shed, a mouse froze in fright as an empty pot rolled across the shelf and came to rest against the wall. All was quiet again and the mouse went on nibbling seeds spilled from the grain sack.

The pot was not entirely empty. It was the snail's winter shelter. Many weeks had passed since it had glided through a gap between rough grey slabs of wood and attached itself to the inside of the pot.

The fall did not break the snail's hold. It drifted in snail sleep, safely sealed inside its shell.

The stars faded and the moon had almost set. Dark shapes became animals, their moist breath making white mist-swirls in the morning air. The cold night wind died and the warm spring breath came with the dawn.

Mist began to rise with the sun. In the far corner of the
farm, the dark bare branches of the cherry tree stood out
against the whiteness. It was at last time for its sap to rise
and its buds to swell and grow.

A finger of sunlight reached through the rough boards of the old wood shed and warmed the snail's shell.

The morning mist lifted from the valley and disappeared into a cloudless blue sky.

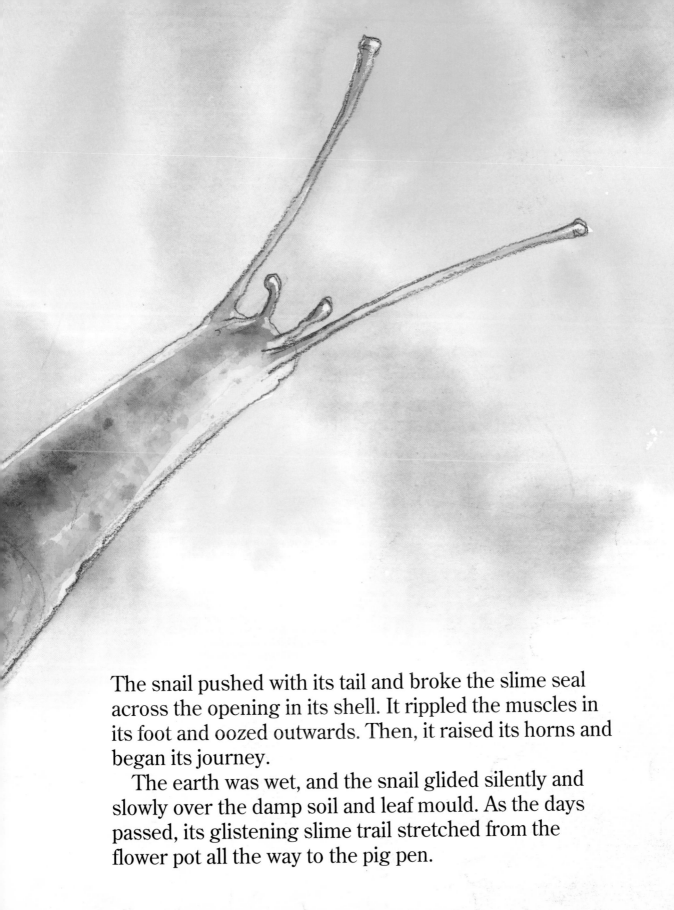

The snail pushed with its tail and broke the slime seal
across the opening in its shell. It rippled the muscles in
its foot and oozed outwards. Then, it raised its horns and
began its journey.

The earth was wet, and the snail glided silently and
slowly over the damp soil and leaf mould. As the days
passed, its glistening slime trail stretched from the
flower pot all the way to the pig pen.

Long shafts of sunlight reached through the pine branches to waken the pig. She moved and grunted, and the piglets squealed for their breakfast.

The pig snuffled happily at the crisp, clear morning and felt the growing warmth of the sun.

'Aaaah,' she sighed and looked down. 'Hello, Snail, where are you going on this fine spring morning?'

The snail stopped and raised its horns. 'Hello, Pig. I am going to wrap myself around the biggest, the reddest, the most beautiful cherry on the cherry tree.'

The pig looked across to the far corner of the farm where the cherry tree stood. 'There are no cherries on the cherry tree yet,' she said.

'There will be when I get there,' said the snail, as it went slowly and calmly gliding along.

The silver trail took the snail over the moist, green grass
to the cow shed. The cow and her calf were lying in the
hay.

'Hello, Snail,' said the cow. 'Where are you going on
this fine, spring day?'

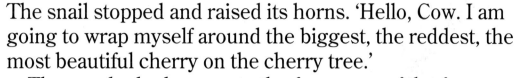

The snail stopped and raised its horns. 'Hello, Cow. I am going to wrap myself around the biggest, the reddest, the most beautiful cherry on the cherry tree.'

The cow looked across to the far corner of the farm where the cherry tree stood. 'There are no cherries on the cherry tree yet,' she said.

'There will be when I get there,' said the snail, as it went slowly and calmly gliding along.

The house dog and cat lay asleep against the rock wall around the herb garden.

The snail's long, slim body glided past, silvery grey in the shadow and with a pearly glow in the late afternoon sunlight. A dry leaf crackled under its weight and the dog opened his eyes. The cat half-opened hers.

'Hello, Snail,' she yawned. 'Where are you going on this fine, sleepy afternoon?'

The snail stopped and raised its horns. 'Hello, Cat. Hello, Dog. I am going to wrap myself around the biggest, the reddest, the most beautiful cherry on the cherry tree.'

The dog stood up and looked across to the far corner of the farm where the cherry tree stood. 'There are no cherries on the cherry tree yet,' he said.

'There will be when I get there,' said the snail, as it went slowly and calmly gliding along.

Parsley grew green and tall in the herb garden. The snail slithered up a stem and began to rasp its teeth over the leaves. Fresh, young lettuces grew nearby and during the night the snail ate steadily. Many other snails came to join the feast – rasping, rasping, rasping.

Early dawnlight shone on the silvery snail-trail patterns all over the cool moist earth beneath the lettuces. The snail crept into a hollow in the rock wall and rested.

The farmer's wife came out of her house to pick some fresh, young beans for lunch. 'Dratted snails,' she muttered. 'I'll get you. See if I don't.'

That night, the farmer and his wife went out into the garden and stomped on all the snails they could find. But they did not find the snail in the hollow in the rock wall.

The hot morning sunshine poured down on the rock
wall. Small lizards skittered over the stones and a large
lizard clumbered up to lie sleeping on the top.
It did not see the small, hidden snail-snack.

Many dry days passed and the farmer watched the sky anxiously for rain clouds. Tiny bronze leaves grew on the cherry tree. Hot winds blew and, as the blossoms fell, tiny cherries began to form.

When the rain came, the children ran out into the field and laughed and jumped for joy.

The duck slop-flapped in the mud and the ducklings began to swim in the puddles as the pond began to fill once more.

The snail came out from its hiding place. It slid slowly down the stones and made its slime trail through the moist leaf-mould under the hedges. The snail's horned head turned from side to side as its foot rippled ever onwards. It kept well away from the duck pond.

Cloud and drizzly rain came with the morning. The grass in the field was long and green and wet. The snail was happy and made good speed.

By late afternoon, the sun had come out and the snail met a big, brown horse and her golden colt. They had eaten their way through the snail-sized raingrass forest.

'Hello, Snail,' said the horse. 'Where are you going?'

'Hello, Horse. Hello, Colt. I am going to wrap myself around the biggest, the reddest, the most beautiful cherry on the cherry tree.'

The horse looked across to the leaf-covered cherry tree. 'There are no cherries on the cherry tree.'

'There will be when I get there,' said the snail, as it went slowly and calmly gliding along.

Storm clouds were gathering again. Birds fell silent. The snail slithered along and arrived at the foot of the cherry tree. A beetle scurried by.

'Hello, Snail. Where are you going on this stormy evening?'

'Hello, Beetle,' said the snail. 'I am going to wrap myself around the biggest, the reddest, the most beautiful cherry on the cherry tree.'

'Well, I don't know about that,' squeaked the beetle. 'When I was up there last, the cherries were small and green and ugly, not big and red and beautiful.'

'They will be when I get there,' said the snail.

Heavy spots of rain began to fall. The snail made its slime seal as it pulled in its head and foot and stuck itself fast to the tree trunk.

It rained and rained and rained.

The wind blew and blew and blew.

In the morning, the sun came out and it shone and shone and shone.

The snail felt the warmth on its shell. It pushed out of its seal and began to climb the cherry tree.

It climbed and climbed and climbed.

The snail climbed until it came to a big, strong branch.
Its foot rippled along and along until at last it came to a
special bunch of cherries. The snail had reached the end
of its journey.

Slowly, the snail's horns touched each cherry in turn.
Then, they moved forward and...

...the snail wrapped itself around the biggest, the reddest, the most beautiful cherry on the cherry tree.